Mr. and Mrs.

DESTINATION

DATE

PLACES TO VISIT

TO DO

TRANSPORTATION
DEPARTURE
ARRIVAL

DEPARTURE
ARRIVAL

DEPARTURE
ARRIVAL

MONEY SPEND

ACCOMMODATION
NAME
BOOKING
ADDRESS
TEL.
ROOM

NOTES

FLIGHT INFORMATION

FLIGHT INFORMATION

AIRLINE:

FLIGHT NUMBER:

DEPARTURE TIME:

ARRIVAL TIME:

FLIGHT INFORMATION

AIRLINE:

FLIGHT NUMBER:

DEPARTURE TIME:

ARRIVAL TIME:

FLIGHT INFORMATION

AIRLINE:

FLIGHT NUMBER:

DEPARTURE TIME:

ARRIVAL TIME:

FLIGHT INFORMATION

AIRLINE:

FLIGHT NUMBER:

DEPARTURE TIME:

ARRIVAL TIME:

FLIGHT INFORMATION

AIRLINE:

FLIGHT NUMBER:

DEPARTURE TIME:

ARRIVAL TIME:

FLIGHT INFORMATION

AIRLINE:

FLIGHT NUMBER:

DEPARTURE TIME:

ARRIVAL TIME:

Personal Expense Tracker

Month:			Year:
Date:	Description Of Expense:	Payment Type:	Amount:

TO-DO LIST

TO-DO LIST

Outfit Planner

Day _____________ Weather _____________

Day Plans _________________________________

Top (s) _________________________________

Bottom _________________________________

Shoes _________________________________

Accessories _________________________________

Night Plans _________________________________

Top (s) _________________________________

Bottom _________________________________

Shoes _________________________________

Accessories _________________________________

Day _____________ Weather _____________

Day Plans _________________________________

Top (s) _________________________________

Bottom _________________________________

Shoes _________________________________

Accessories _________________________________

Night Plans _________________________________

Top (s) _________________________________

Bottom _________________________________

Shoes _________________________________

Accessories _________________________________

Day _____________ Weather _____________

Day Plans _________________________________

Top (s) _________________________________

Bottom _________________________________

Shoes _________________________________

Accessories _________________________________

Night Plans _________________________________

Top (s) _________________________________

Bottom _________________________________

Shoes _________________________________

Accessories _________________________________

Day _____________ Weather _____________

Day Plans _________________________________

Top (s) _________________________________

Bottom _________________________________

Shoes _________________________________

Accessories _________________________________

Night Plans _________________________________

Top (s) _________________________________

Bottom _________________________________

Shoes _________________________________

Accessories _________________________________

Outfit Planner

Day _____________ Weather_____________

Day Plans _______________________

Top (s)_________________________

Bottom _________________________

Shoes _________________________

Accessories_____________________

Night Plans_____________________

Top (s) ________________________

Bottom ________________________

Shoes _________________________

Accessories ____________________

Day _____________ Weather_____________

Day Plans _______________________

Top (s)_________________________

Bottom _________________________

Shoes _________________________

Accessories_____________________

Night Plans_____________________

Top (s) ________________________

Bottom ________________________

Shoes _________________________

Accessories ____________________

Day _____________ Weather_____________

Day Plans _______________________

Top (s)_________________________

Bottom _________________________

Shoes _________________________

Accessories_____________________

Night Plans_____________________

Top (s) ________________________

Bottom ________________________

Shoes _________________________

Accessories ____________________

Day _____________ Weather_____________

Day Plans _______________________

Top (s)_________________________

Bottom _________________________

Shoes _________________________

Accessories_____________________

Night Plans_____________________

Top (s) ________________________

Bottom ________________________

Shoes _________________________

Accessories ____________________

Remember to ...

Monday	Tuesday

Wednesday	Thursday

Friday	Saturday

Sunday

Notes:

Monday

- ☐ _______________________
- ☐ _______________________
- ☐ _______________________
- ☐ _______________________

Tuesday

- ☐ _______________________
- ☐ _______________________
- ☐ _______________________
- ☐ _______________________

Wednesday

- ☐ _______________________
- ☐ _______________________
- ☐ _______________________
- ☐ _______________________

Thursday

- ☐ _______________________
- ☐ _______________________
- ☐ _______________________
- ☐ _______________________

Friday

- ☐ _______________________
- ☐ _______________________
- ☐ _______________________
- ☐ _______________________

Saturday

- ☐ _______________________
- ☐ _______________________
- ☐ _______________________
- ☐ _______________________

Sunday

- ☐ _______________________
- ☐ _______________________
- ☐ _______________________
- ☐ _______________________

Notes: _______________________________________

____

____

____

Attach stickers and postcards here

Attach stickers and postcards here

Attach stickers and postcards here

Attach stickers and postcards here

Attach stickers and postcards here

Wine

Vintage

grapes

% alcohol

producer

country-region

perfect pairing

serving temperature

suggested glass

price

wine-tasting

when

where

with

appearance

nose

taste

opinion

notes and additional thoughts

rating:

Wine

Vintage

grapes

% alcohol

producer

country-region

perfect pairing

serving temperature

suggested glass

price

wine-tasting

when

where

with

appearance

nose

taste

opinion

notes and additional thoughts

rating:

COFFEE NAME _______________________   DATE _______________

BEVERAGE _______________________

PLACE TASTED _______________________   PRICE _______________

COUNTRY / REGION _______________________

COMPANY _______________________

TESTING RATING

	0.5	1	1.5	2	2.5	3	3.5	4	4.5	5
APPEARANCE										
AROMA										
FLAVOR										

	0.5	1	1.5	2	2.5	3	3.5	4	4.5	5
SWEET										
ACIDIC										
SPICY										
CITRUS										
CHOCOLATE										
CARAMEL										
BITTER										
SAVORY										

BREW METHOD

DRIP ☐   ESPRESSO ☐   PRESS ☐

POUR-OVER ☐   SIPHON ☐   OTHER _______

NOTES _______________________

____
____
____
____
____
____
____

RECOMMEND TO _______________________

____
____
____
____
____
____
____

COFFEE NAME _______________________   DATE _______________

BEVERAGE _______________________________

PLACE TASTED _______________________   PRICE _______________

COUNTRY / REGION _______________________

COMPANY _______________________________

TESTING RATING

	0.5	1	1.5	2	2.5	3	3.5	4	4.5	5
APPEARANCE										
AROMA										
FLAVOR										

	0.5	1	1.5	2	2.5	3	3.5	4	4.5	5
SWEET										
ACIDIC										
SPICY										
CITRUS										
CHOCOLATE										
CARAMEL										
BITTER										
SAVORY										

BREW METHOD

DRIP ☐   ESPRESSO ☐   PRESS ☐

POUR-OVER ☐   SIPHON ☐   OTHER _______

NOTES _______________________

____

____

____

____

____

____

____

____

RECOMMEND TO _______________________

____

____

____

____

____

____

____

COFFEE NAME _______________________   DATE _______________

BEVERAGE _______________________

PLACE TASTED _______________________   PRICE _______________

COUNTRY / REGION _______________________

COMPANY _______________________

TESTING RATING

	0.5	1	1.5	2	2.5	3	3.5	4	4.5	5
APPEARANCE										
AROMA										
FLAVOR										

	0.5	1	1.5	2	2.5	3	3.5	4	4.5	5
SWEET										
ACIDIC										
SPICY										
CITRUS										
CHOCOLATE										
CARAMEL										
BITTER										
SAVORY										

BREW METHOD

DRIP ☐   ESPRESSO ☐   PRESS ☐

POUR-OVER ☐   SIPHON ☐   OTHER _______

NOTES _______________________

____

____

____

____

____

____

____

RECOMMEND TO _______________________

____

____

____

____

____

____

____

COFFEE NAME _________________________ DATE _____________

BEVERAGE _________________________________

PLACE TASTED _____________________ PRICE _________

COUNTRY / REGION _______________________

COMPANY _________________________________

TESTING RATING

	0.5 1 1.5 2 2.5 3 3.5 4 4.5 5
APPEARANCE	☐☐☐☐☐☐☐☐☐☐
AROMA	☐☐☐☐☐☐☐☐☐☐
FLAVOR	☐☐☐☐☐☐☐☐☐☐

	0.5 1 1.5 2 2.5 3 3.5 4 4.5 5
SWEET	☐☐☐☐☐☐☐☐☐☐
ACIDIC	☐☐☐☐☐☐☐☐☐☐
SPICY	☐☐☐☐☐☐☐☐☐☐
CITRUS	☐☐☐☐☐☐☐☐☐☐
CHOCOLATE	☐☐☐☐☐☐☐☐☐☐
CARAMEL	☐☐☐☐☐☐☐☐☐☐
BITTER	☐☐☐☐☐☐☐☐☐☐
SAVORY	☐☐☐☐☐☐☐☐☐☐

BREW METHOD

DRIP ☐ ESPRESSO ☐ PRESS ☐

POUR-OVER ☐ SIPHON ☐ OTHER _______

NOTES _________________________

____

____

____

____

____

____

____

____

RECOMMEND TO _______________

____

____

____

____

____

____

____

____

Scuba

Dive Number: _________________

Date: _____________________

Location: _________________

Ocean: ___________________

TIME IN:	TIME OUT:

Bar / psi START	Bar / psi END

GEAR USED

BCD: _____________________

Wetsuit: _________________

Fins: ___________________

Weights: _____________ **kg/lbs**

Cylinder: _____________ **Litres**

☐ **Steel**   ☐ **Aluminium**

☐ **Fresh**   ☐ **Salt**   ☐ **Shore**   ☐ **Boat**   ☐ **Drift**   ☐ **Night**   ☐ **Training**

Dive Comments:

____

____

____

____

____

SI   PG   PG

☐ Computer Dive   BOTTOM TIME

DEPTH

RNT_______
ABT _______
TBT _______

VISIBILITY:

____

TEMP: Air _____ Surface _____ Bottom _____

DIVE SHOP STAMP

BOTTOM TIME TO DATE: _____________

Time Of This Dive: _____________

Cumulative Dive Time: _____________

Verification Signature:

____

☐ **Instructor** ☐ **Divemaster** ☐ **Buddy**

Certification No: _____________

Dive Number: ___________________

Date: _______________________

Location: _________________

Ocean: ___________________

TIME IN:	TIME OUT:

Bar / psi START	Bar / psi END

GEAR USED

BCD: ___________________

Wetsuit: ___________________

Fins: ___________________

Weights: ___________ **kg/lbs**

Cylinder: ___________ **Litres**

☐ **Steel**   ☐ **Aluminium**

☐ **Fresh**   ☐ **Salt**   ☐ **Shore**   ☐ **Boat**   ☐ **Drift**   ☐ **Night**   ☐ **Training**

Dive Comments:

____

____

____

____

____

SI   PG   PG

☐ Computer Dive   BOTTOM TIME

DEPTH

RNT_______
ABT _______
TBT _______

VISIBILITY:

____

TEMP: Air _____ Surface _____ Bottom _____

DIVE SHOP STAMP

BOTTOM TIME TO DATE: ___________

Time Of This Dive: ___________

Cumulative Dive Time: ___________

Verification Signature:

____

☐ **Instructor** ☐ **Divemaster** ☐ **Buddy**

Certification No: ___________

Recipes to bring home

RECIPE:

DIFFICULTY: RATING: PREP TIME: COOK TIME:

INGREDIENTS:

COOKING INSTRUCTIONS:

PORTIONS:

SERVE WITH:

ALLERGENS:

☐ MILK
☐ FISH
☐ EGGS
☐ LUPIN
☐ CELERY
☐ PEANUTS
☐ MUSTARD
☐ MOLLUSCS
☐ TREE NUTS
☐ SOYBEANS
☐ CRUSTACEANS
☐ SESAME SEEDS
☐ CEREALS CONTAINING GLUTEN
☐ SULPHUR DIOXIDE AND SULPHITES

NOTES:

RECIPE:

DIFFICULTY: RATING: PREP TIME: COOK TIME:

INGREDIENTS:

____

____

____

____

____

____

____

____

____

____

____

____

____

____

____

PORTIONS:
SERVE WITH:

COOKING INSTRUCTIONS:

ALLERGENS:

☐ MILK
☐ FISH
☐ EGGS
☐ LUPIN
☐ CELERY
☐ PEANUTS
☐ MUSTARD
☐ MOLLUSCS
☐ TREE NUTS
☐ SOYBEANS
☐ CRUSTACEANS
☐ SESAME SEEDS
☐ CEREALS CONTAINING GLUTEN
☐ SULPHUR DIOXIDE AND SULPHITES

NOTES:

RECIPE:

DIFFICULTY: RATING: PREP TIME: COOK TIME:

INGREDIENTS:

COOKING INSTRUCTIONS:

PORTIONS:

SERVE WITH:

ALLERGENS:

- ☐ MILK
- ☐ FISH
- ☐ EGGS
- ☐ LUPIN
- ☐ CELERY
- ☐ PEANUTS
- ☐ MUSTARD
- ☐ MOLLUSCS
- ☐ TREE NUTS
- ☐ SOYBEANS
- ☐ CRUSTACEANS
- ☐ SESAME SEEDS
- ☐ CEREALS CONTAINING GLUTEN
- ☐ SULPHUR DIOXIDE AND SULPHITES

NOTES:

RECIPE:

DIFFICULTY: RATING: PREP TIME: COOK TIME:

INGREDIENTS:

PORTIONS:

SERVE WITH:

COOKING INSTRUCTIONS:

ALLERGENS:

- ☐ MILK
- ☐ FISH
- ☐ EGGS
- ☐ LUPIN
- ☐ CELERY
- ☐ PEANUTS
- ☐ MUSTARD
- ☐ MOLLUSCS
- ☐ TREE NUTS
- ☐ SOYBEANS
- ☐ CRUSTACEANS
- ☐ SESAME SEEDS
- ☐ CEREALS CONTAINING GLUTEN
- ☐ SULPHUR DIOXIDE AND SULPHITES

NOTES:

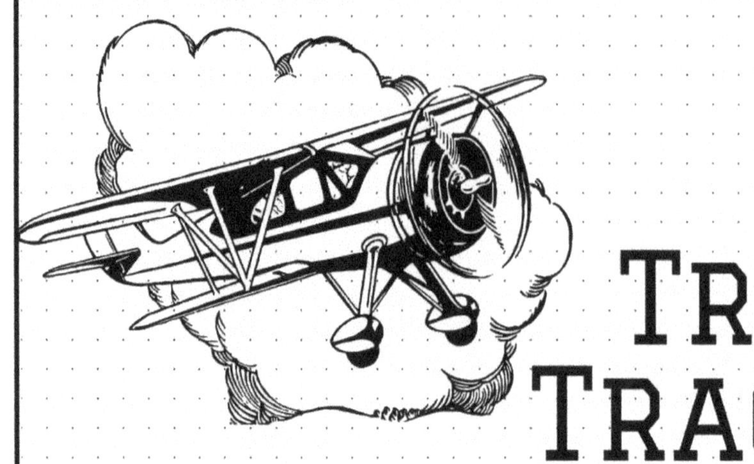

TRAVEL TRACKER

WHERE I'VE BEEN...

WHERE I WANT TO GO NEXT

THIS OR THAT

TRAVEL EDITION

CITY / BEACH

MORNING / NIGHTTIME

DINNER / COCKTAILS

EUROPE / ASIA

LUXURY / BACKPACKING

RESTAURANT / STREET FOOD

PLANE / BOAT

PLANNING / IMPROVISE

SUN / SNOW

SHOPPING / ATTRACTIONS

Travel Log

Travel Log Journal

Travel Log Journal

Travel Log Journal

Travel Log Journal

Travel Log Journal

Favorite Restaurant

Favorite Restaurant

Favorite Restaurant

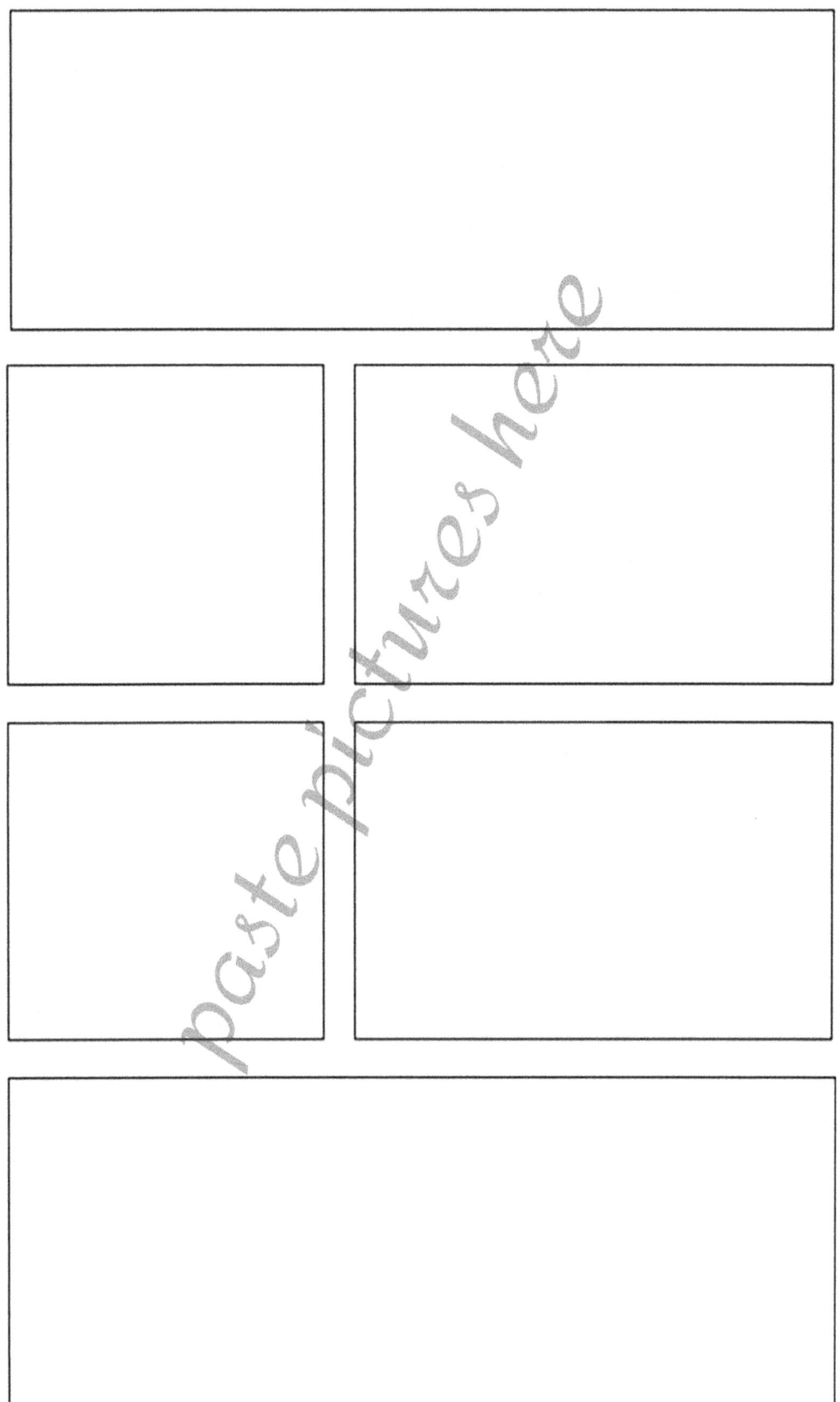

paste pictures here

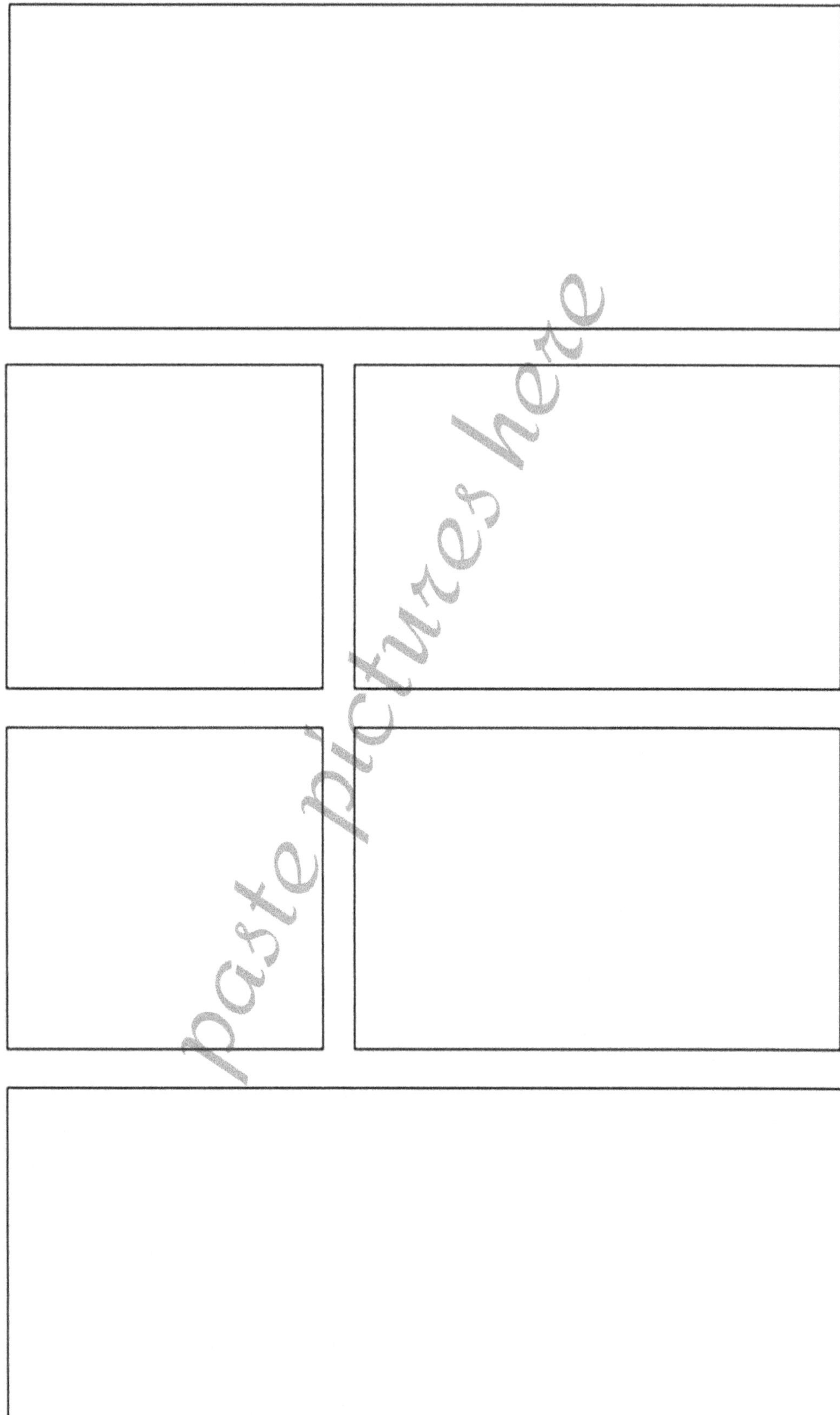

paste pictures here

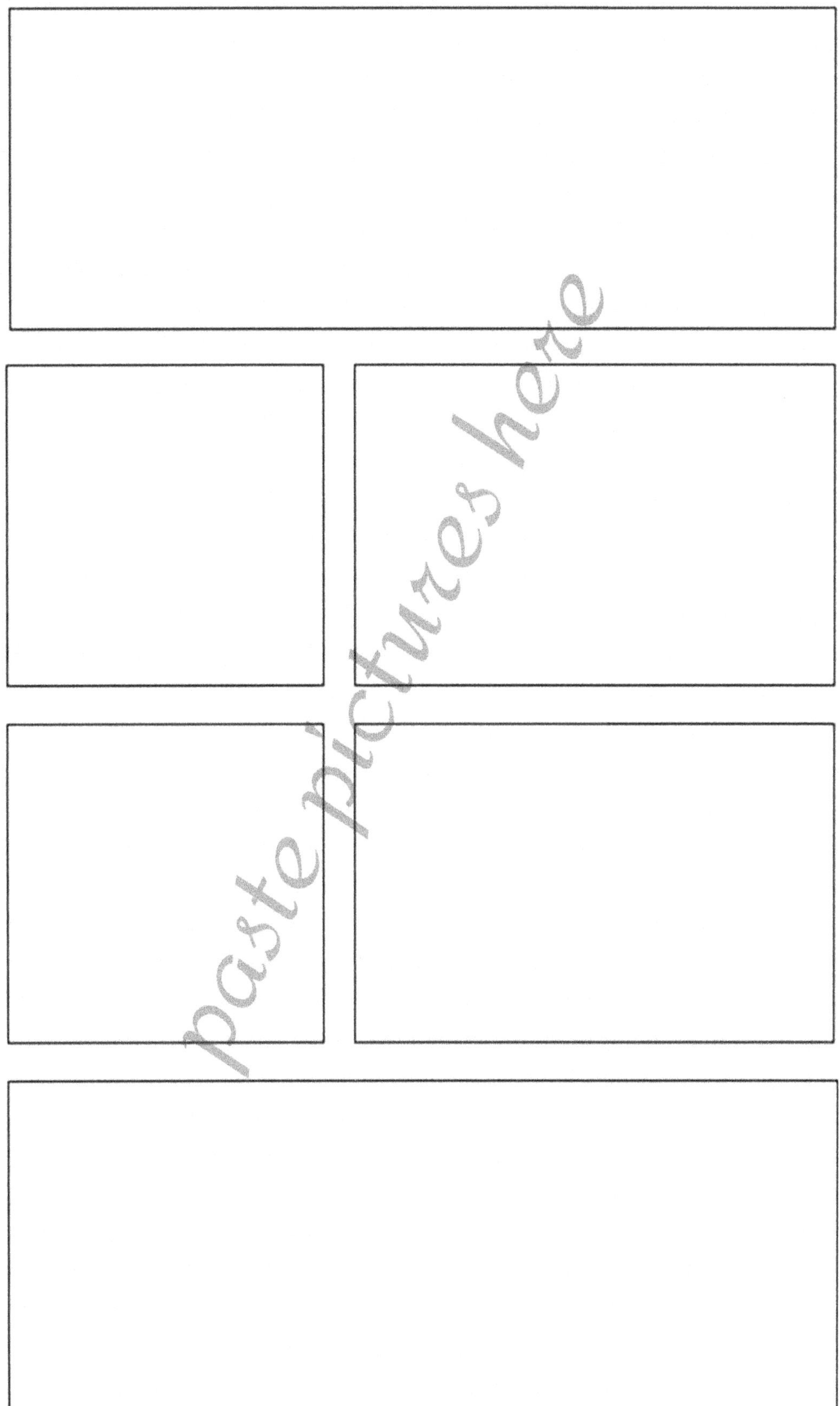
paste pictures here

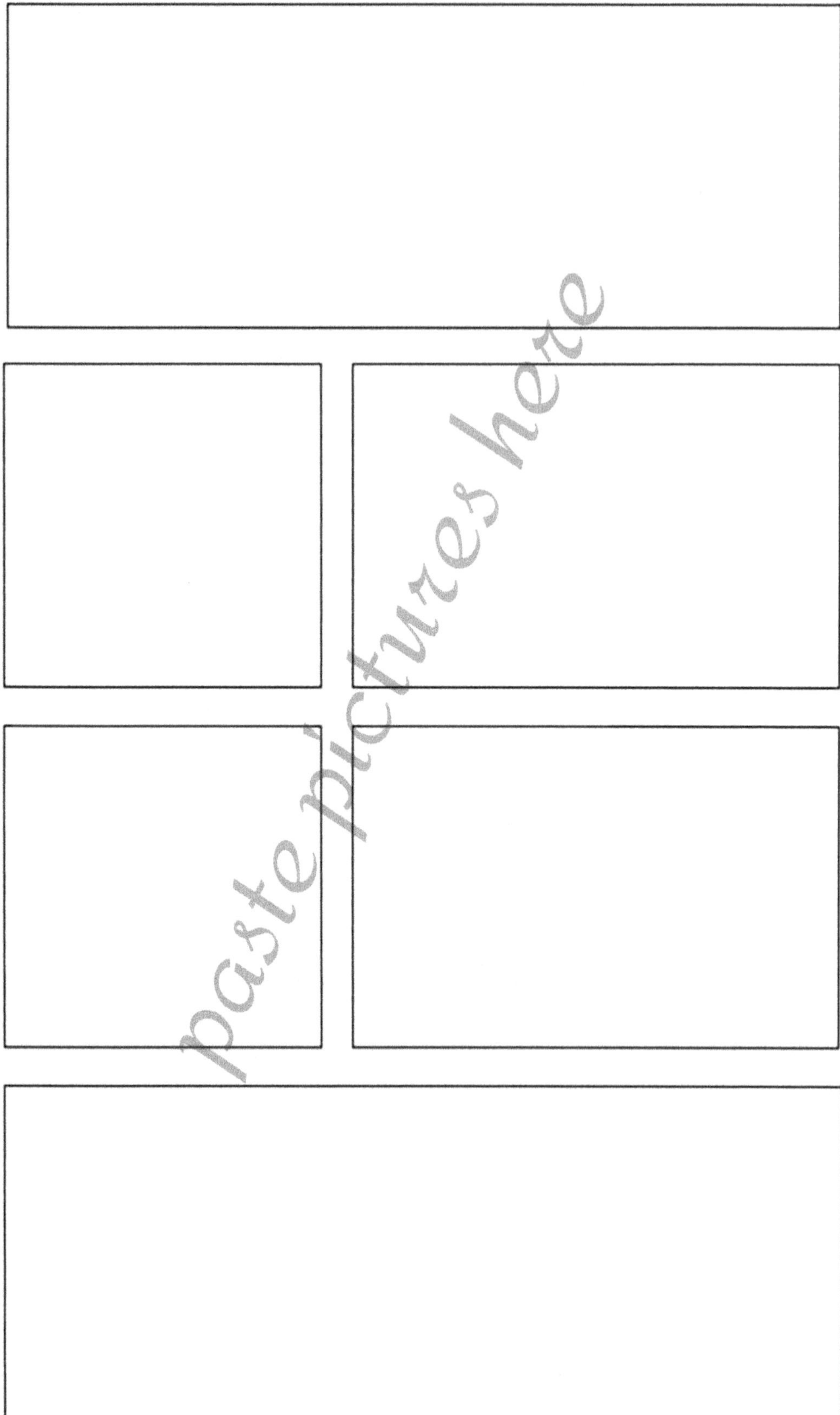

paste pictures here

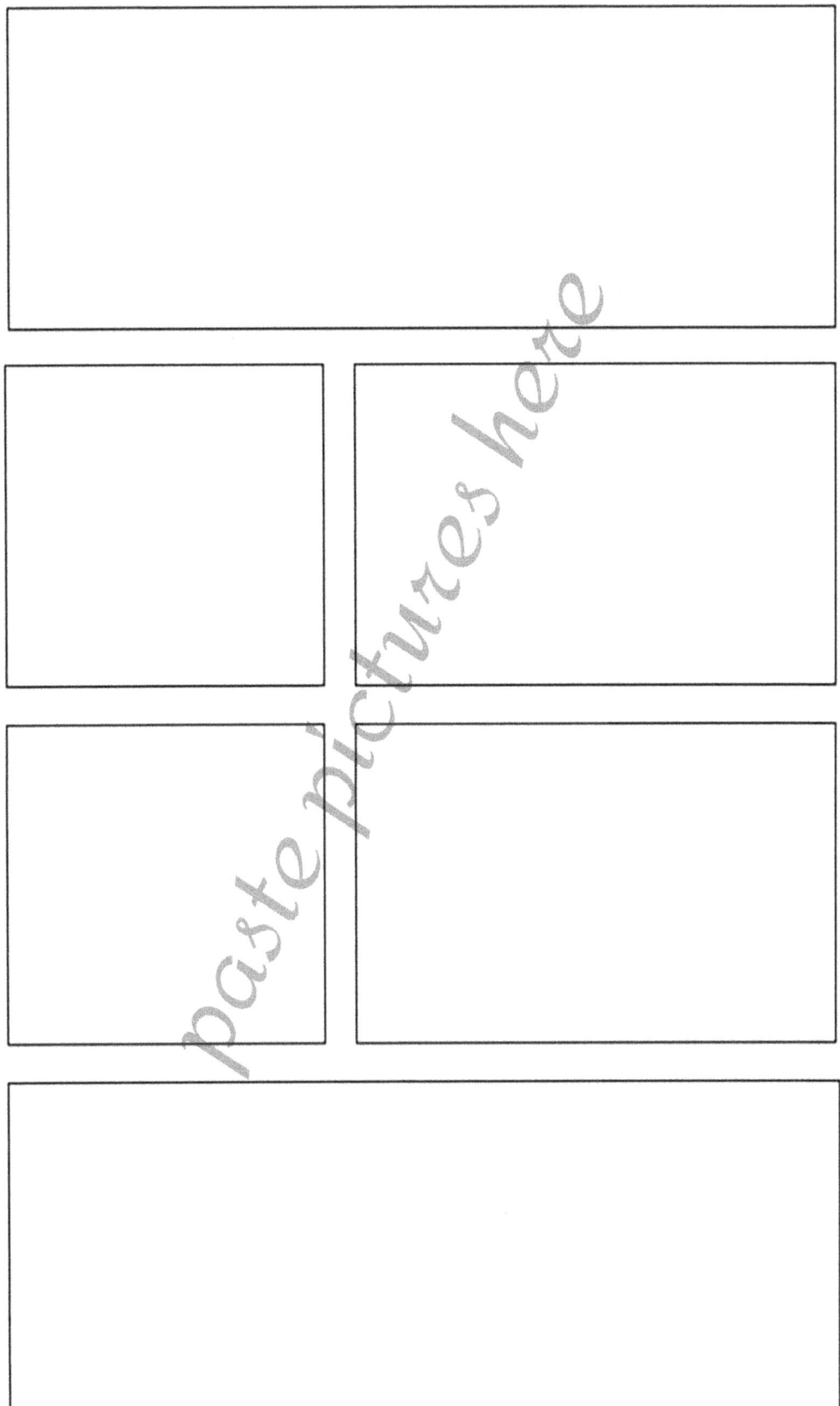
paste pictures here

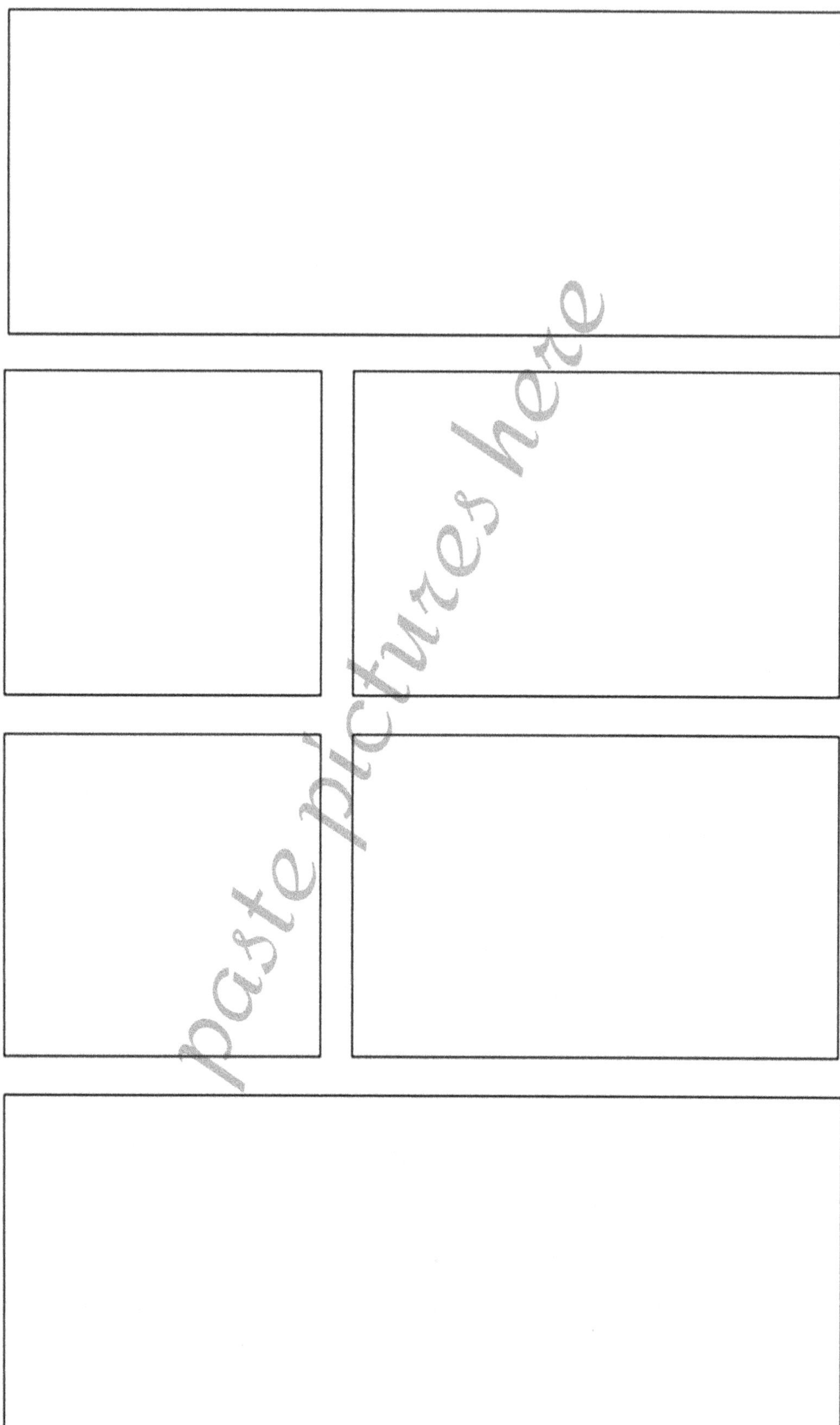

paste pictures here

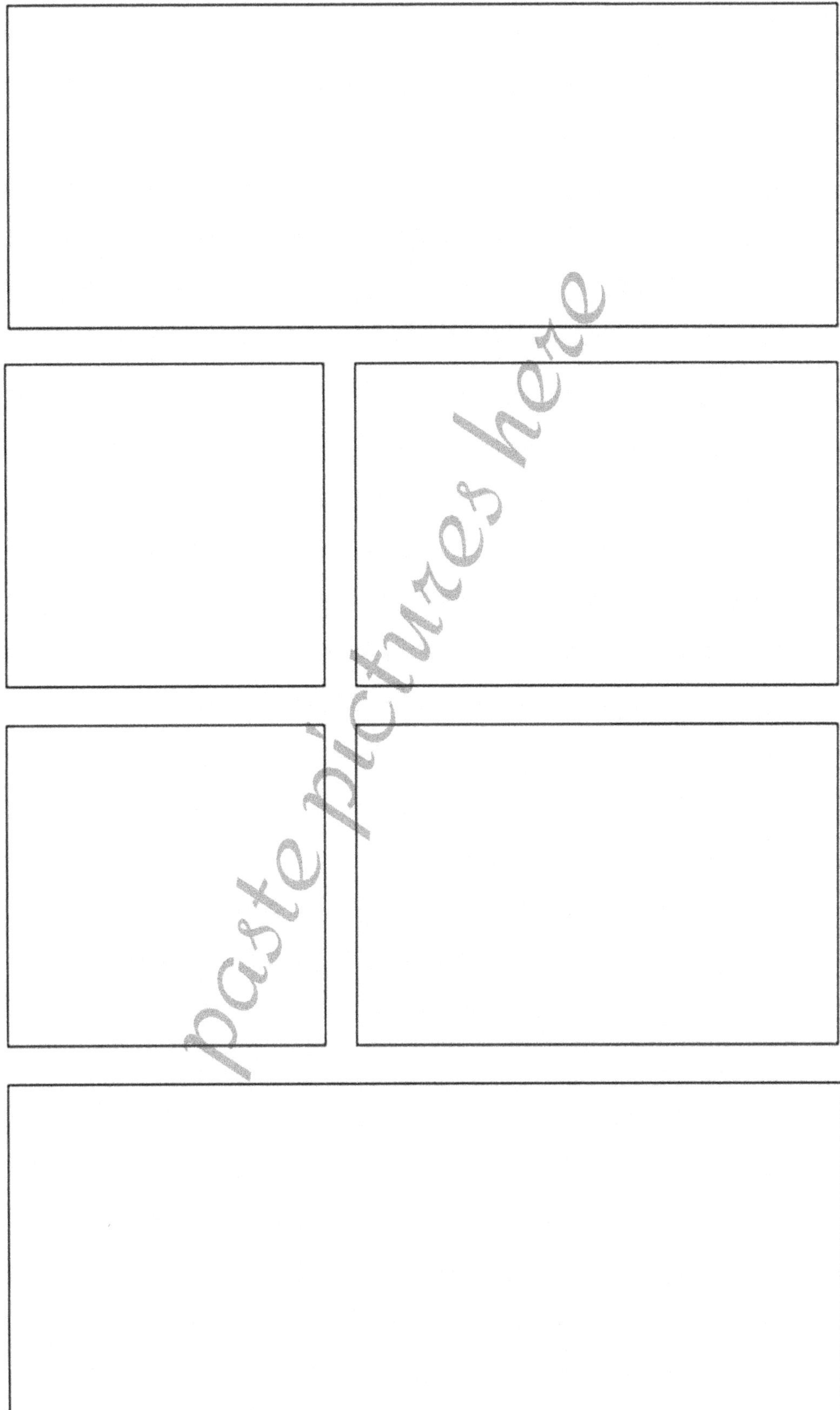
paste pictures here

TRIP WEATHER LOG

TRIP WEATHER LOG

TRIP WEATHER LOG

TRIP WEATHER LOG

TRIP WEATHER LOG

Sketch me,
paste, free write
me

Our Hotel

Relax
Refresh
Reconnect

Places we visited

Toes in the sand

From Here to There

From Here to
There

add notes, pictures, or postcards

Add notes, pictures, or postcards

add notes, pictures, or postcards

add notes, pictures, or postcards

Add notes, pictures, or postcards

add notes, pictures, or postcards

·ITALIA·ITALY·
ISTANBUL
AIR MA
AN POSTA

I Love you

Just married

Special Moments

I'M
YOURS

Notes

Notes

Notes

Notes

Notes

Notes

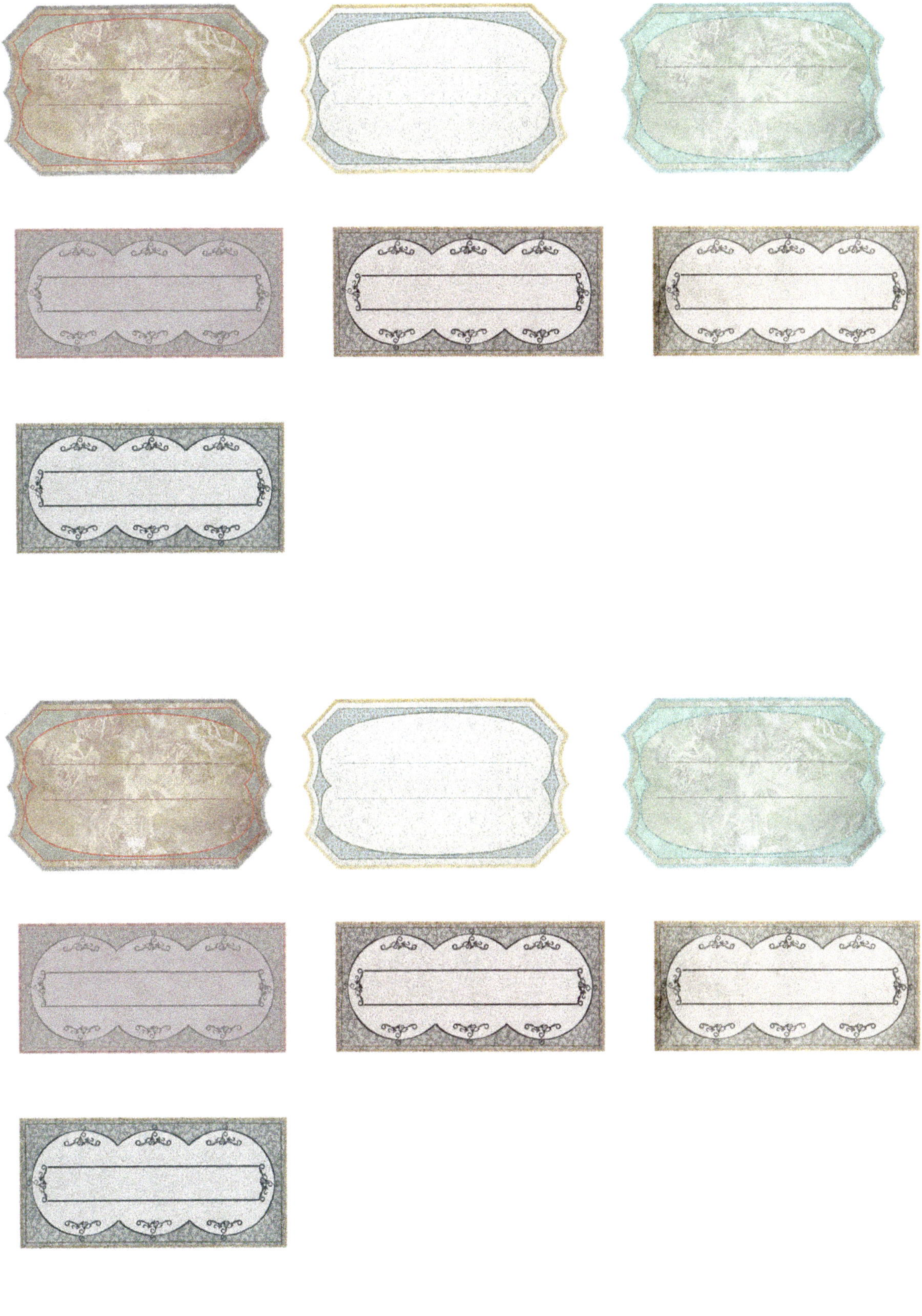

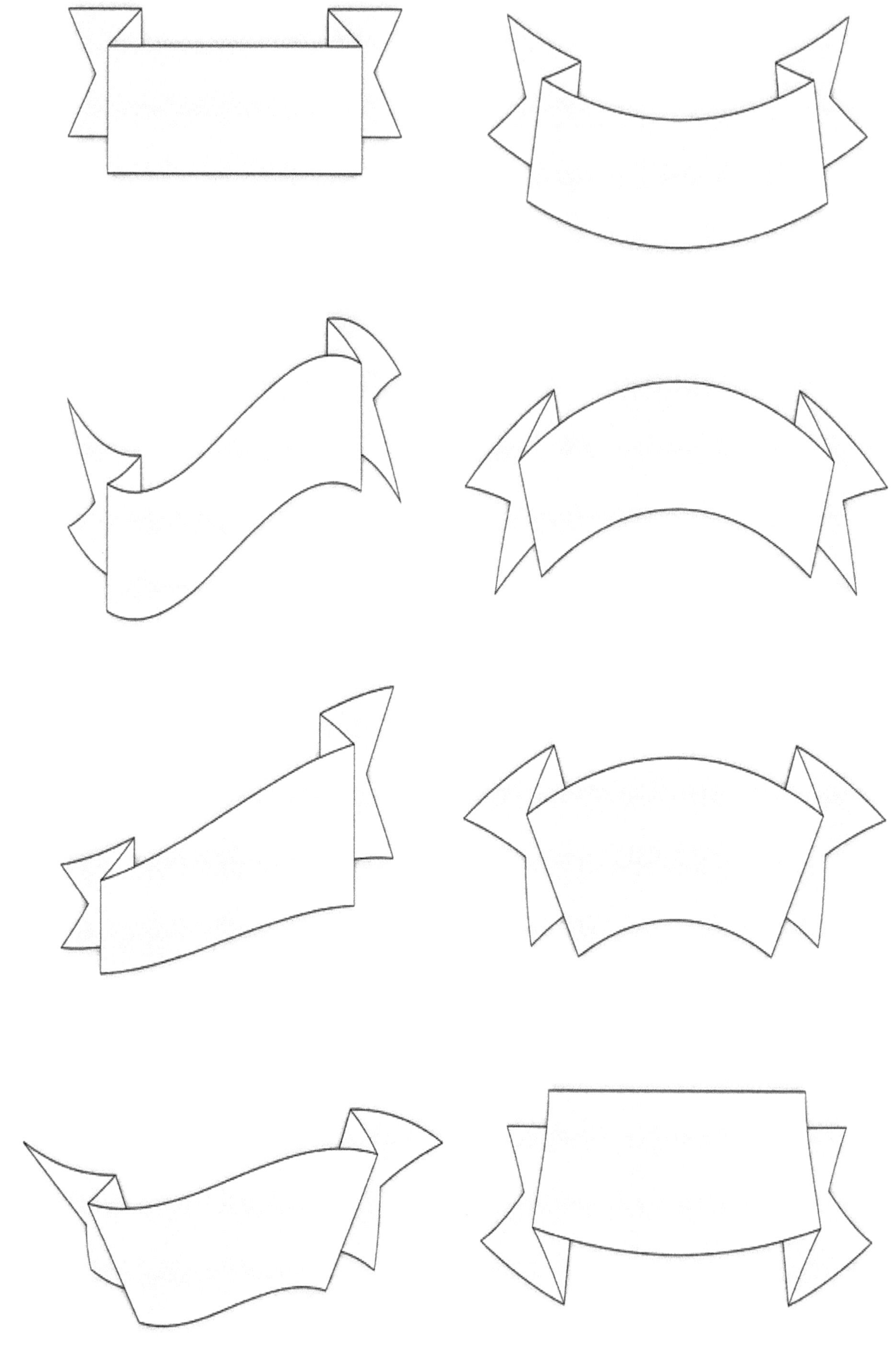

you got this.

TICKET
123456
TICKET
23456
POP
CORN

Tbrad Designs